HOW ARE THEY DIFFERENT?

Tell Me the DIFFERENCE Between a

PORCUPINE
and a HEDGEHOG

Leigh Rockwood

PowerKiDS press™

New York

Published in 2013 by The Rosen Publishing Group, Inc.
29 East 21st Street, New York, NY 10010

First Edition

Editor: Joanne Randolph
Book Design: Kate Laczynski

Photo Credits: Cover (porcupine) Juergen & Christine Sohns/Picture Press/Getty Images; cover (hedgehog) Tim Melling/Flickr/Getty Images; p. 4 Philippe Henry/Oxford Scientific/Getty Images; p. 5 Jeroen Visser/Shutterstock.com; p. 6 Gary Omblar/Dorling Kindersley/Getty Images; p. 7 B. Stefanov/Shutterstock.com; p. 8 Richard J. Green/Photo Researchers/Getty Images; p. 9 Justin Sullivan/Getty Images News/Getty Images; p. 10 MikeE/Shutterstock.com; p. 11 Anneka/Shutterstock.com; p. 12 © iStockphoto.com/Valerie Mellema; p. 13 © iStockphoto.com/Alonzo Aranda; p. 14 © iStockphoto.com/Molly DeLong; p. 15 iStockphoto/Thinkstock; p. 16 Tony Rix/Shutterstock.com; p. 17 Jonathan Gale/Oxford Scientific/Getty Images; p. 18 Design Pics/Thinkstock; p. 19 Les Stocker/Oxford Scientific/Getty Images; p. 20 Don Johnston/All Canada Photos/Getty Images; p. 21 Otto & Irmgard Hahn/Picture Press/Getty Images; p. 22 James Hager/Robert Harding World Imagery/Getty Images.

Library of Congress Cataloging-in-Publication Data

Rockwood, Leigh.
Tell me the difference between a porcupine and a hedgehog / by Leigh Rockwood. — 1st ed.
    p. cm. — (How are they different?)
Includes index.
ISBN 978-1-4488-9637-0 (library binding) — ISBN 978-1-4488-9732-2 (pbk.) — ISBN 978-1-4488-9733-9 (6-pack)
1. Porcupines—Juvenile literature. 2. Hedgehogs—Juvenile literature. I. Title.
QL737.R652R63 2013
599.35'97—dc23
                                    2012020399

Manufactured in the United States of America
CPSIA Compliance Information: Batch #W13PK5: For Further Information contact Rosen Publishing, New York, New York at 1-800-237-9932

CONTENTS

LET'S LOOK AT PORCUPINES AND HEDGEHOGS

Porcupines and hedgehogs are two **mammals** that look a lot alike at first glance. Both animals **defend** themselves from enemies using sharp spines or quills. Even their names point out that they both have features that remind people of pigs. "Porcupine" comes from the Latin words for "quill pig," while hedgehogs

The porcupines in North and South America like to climb trees, while the species on other continents generally stay on the ground.

4

Hedgehogs make a piglike grunt while they search for food, which is one of the reasons they got their name.

got their name for the piglike way they nose through bushes.

Once you get past their spiny hides, though, you will see that these two animals are not that closely related. Porcupines and hedgehogs live in different places and have different diets and behaviors. This book will teach you more about these two prickly animals.

TWO DIFFERENT FAMILIES

Scientists classify, or group, living things based on how they are alike. A **species** is one kind of living thing. An order is a larger grouping of different species that have things in common with one another.

Porcupines are rodents, and like other rodents their teeth grow throughout their lives. Porcupines chew tree bark and other plant matter to keep their teeth short.

Although porcupines and hedgehogs are both classified as mammals, they belong to different orders. The 23 species of porcupines belong to the rodent order. Squirrels, mice, and beavers are rodents, too. The 16 species of hedgehogs belong to an order called Erinaceomorpha. Hedgehogs and gymnures are members of this order.

HOW ARE PORCUPINES AND HEDGEHOGS ALIKE?

Because they are so distantly related, porcupines and hedgehogs do not have many things in common besides their prickly-looking bodies. Both animals are generally small to medium sized. The North American porcupine's

This prehensile-tailed porcupine of South America has white-tipped fur and spines. Its name refers to the fact that its tail can grab hold of branches as it climbs.

This hedgehog has white tips on its fur and spines, too. That is about all it has in common with the porcupine on the facing page, though!

body can be from 2 to 3 feet (60–90 cm) long with a 10-inch (25 cm) tail. This porcupine can weigh between 10 and 35 pounds (4.5–16 kg).

Hedgehogs are smaller than porcupines. A typical European hedgehog's body is up to 1 foot (30 cm) long with a 2-inch (5 cm) tail. It can weigh up to 2.5 pounds (1 kg).

QUILLS AND SPINES

When a porcupine thinks it is in danger, it uses muscles in its skin to make its quills stand out. The porcupine cannot shoot the quills, but they do break off easily.

Although porcupines and hedgehogs look like they have similar prickly parts, they are quite different! Porcupines have quills, while hedgehogs have spines. A porcupine has up to 30,000 quills. These quills generally lie flat unless the animal feels threatened. Then it makes its quills stand out from its body.

Hedgehogs have thick layers of around 5,000 spines on their backs and sides. These spines always stick out from their bodies, making them look and feel like pincushions that are full of pins. One thing spines and quills have in common is that they are made up of the same stuff as your hair and nails.

While most of a porcupine's hair is soft, this is not true of hedgehogs. All the fur on their backs and sides feels hard and prickly.

COMPARING PORCUPINES

SCIENTIFIC ORDER	Rodentia
NUMBER OF SPECIES	23
SHARP PARTS	Quills
NUMBER OF SHARP PARTS	30,000 quills
DIET	Herbivore
MOST ACTIVE	Night
RANGE	The Americas, Europe, Asia, and Africa
LIFE SPAN	15 years (wild), 20 years (zoo)

and HEDGEHOGS

Erinaceomorpha	**SCIENTIFIC ORDER**
16	**NUMBER OF SPECIES**
Spines	**SHARP PARTS**
5,000 spines	**NUMBER OF SHARP PARTS**
Omnivore	**DIET**
Night	**MOST ACTIVE**
Europe, Asia, Africa	**RANGE**
8 years (wild), 10 years (zoo)	**LIFE SPAN**

DIFFERENT DEFENSES

Porcupines and hedgehogs use their spiky bodies to defend themselves from **predators** in different ways. While it is a myth that a porcupine can shoot its quills, they come out easily and barbs on the end make a quill difficult and painful to remove. When a quill detaches from a porcupine's body, a new one grows to replace it.

This dog likely wishes it had never seen the porcupine that left these quills in its mouth and snout.

When in danger, hedgehogs roll into a tight ball, as this one has done.

Hedgehogs defend themselves by curling up into a spiny ball. They use their muscles and extra skin to tuck their heads and legs into their bodies and to protect their soft bellies. Although porcupines and hedgehogs use their defenses differently, they both send the message to stay away!

DIFFERENT DIETS

Porcupines and hedgehogs also differ in the kinds of foods they eat. Porcupines are **herbivores**, meaning they eat only plants. Depending on where they live, they will eat tree bark, nuts, fruit, leaves, and whatever other plant matter they can find. As do other

Porcupines eat many different kinds of plants and plant matter. This porcupine is enjoying some berries.

This hedgehog is eating a snail it has found. It was once thought that hedgehogs ate mainly insects, but scientists now know their diet is much more varied.

rodents, porcupines have front teeth that are always growing. They **gnaw** on wood or even bones to keep these teeth sharp.

Hedgehogs are **omnivores**, which means that they eat both plants and animals. In addition to seeds and other plant matter, they eat snails, slugs, bugs, and worms. Some people welcome the sight of hedgehogs in their garden because they eat many garden pests.

PORCUPINE AND HEDGEHOG HABITATS

Scientists divide porcupines into **Old World** and **New World** porcupines. Old World porcupines live in Europe, Asia, and Africa, while New World porcupines live in North America, Central America, and South America.

Some New World porcupines live in deciduous or evergreen forests.

This European hedgehog makes its home in a tree hollow.

Both Old World and New World porcupines may live in forest, grassland, or even desert **habitats**. Hedgehogs are found in Europe, Asia, and Africa, where they make their homes by building nests, digging burrows in the ground, or taking over burrows other animals have left behind. Like porcupines, hedgehogs can be found in a wide variety of habitats, such as grasslands, forests, deserts, and even backyard gardens.

As do other mammals, porcupine and hedgehog mothers give birth to live young after **mating**. Porcupine mothers generally have one to three babies, called porcupettes. Hedgehog mothers typically have four to seven babies, called hoglets.

Porcupettes find their own food with help from their mothers when they are just a few days old. They stay with their mothers for about six months.

20

Hoglets stay with their mothers for about six weeks before striking out on their own.

Porcupettes have quills when they are born. Hoglets have spines at birth, too. In both animals, these prickly parts are soft and flexible when they are born. They become hard and sharp soon after they are born, though. Both animals drink their mothers' milk until they are old enough to go **foraging** with their mothers. Once they are big enough to take care of themselves, the porcupine and hedgehog young strike out on their own.

Now you know about the many differences between porcupines and hedgehogs. If you visit a zoo, you might be able to see a porcupine exhibit. You might even be able to meet a hedgehog up close! Hedgehogs are not listed as **endangered**, but two species of porcupines are listed as **vulnerable** due to habitat loss. People who study these animals are working to protect these porcupines and their habitats, though.

A baby porcupine.

GLOSSARY

defend (dih-FEND) To guard from being hurt.

endangered (in-DAYN-jerd) In danger of no longer living.

foraging (FOR-ij-ing) Hunting or searching for something.

gnaw (NAW) To keep on biting something.

habitats (HA-buh-tats) The surroundings where animals or plants naturally live.

herbivores (ER-buh-vorz) Animals that eat only plants.

mammals (MA-mulz) Warm-blooded animals that have backbones and hair, breathe air, and feed milk to their young.

mating (MAYT-ing) Coming together to make babies.

New World (NOO WURLD) North America and South America.

Old World (OHLD WURLD) The part of the world that includes Asia, Africa, and Europe.

omnivores (OM-nih-vorz) Animals that eat both plants and animals.

predators (PREH-duh-terz) Animals that kill other animals for food.

species (SPEE-sheez) One kind of living thing. All people are one species.

vulnerable (VUL-neh-reh-bul) Open to being hurt or becoming extinct.

INDEX

WEBSITES

Due to the changing nature of Internet links, PowerKids Press has developed an online list of websites related to the subject of this book. This site is updated regularly. Please use this link to access the list: www.powerkidslinks.com/hatd/pohe/